100 Free Ways To Happier Days~ .

This book has been inspired by the
over the years who have had questi   y
school and moving up to secondary   ...nts, tips,
ideas or things to think about to help   _...ident and ready for
the next exciting step in their lives.

Thanks to all the lovely people who have taken time to let me know the concerns that their children have about starting secondary school. You have been a great help.

1. Getting To Know Your New Teachers

Some pupils worry about going to secondary school because they will need to get to know their new teachers and they think it might be hard for their teachers to get to know them.

When you go to secondary school, you usually have different teachers for different lessons but you often have a form tutor who sees you every day and will get to know you really well.

Why not write them a letter telling them about yourself? The letter could contain anything you really want to ask, and it can also tell the tutor anything you want them to know about you. This can be a great way to begin to feel more confident that your tutor will know what they need to know about you from the first day.

2. Getting Lost On The First Day

Some pupils worry that they will get lost on their first day. They realise that it will be bigger in their secondary school. The school may have a map or plan of the school that they can give you to help you find your way around. If not, perhaps you can design your own after going on a school visit. You could make a rough stretch of the school and label the parts that you really want to remember. Having a map to help you get around can really help you feel less worried about getting lost!

3. Design A Classroom

You may get the chance to visit your classroom before the first day of term. If you do, you can make a sketch of the classroom to help you to remember where everything is. It can be fun to design your own ideal classroom. What would you include in your ideal classroom? Thinking about new places in this way can help to reassure you that while your new classroom may look different it will have all the things you need in it. You will soon get used to where everything is and many classrooms have the important things labelled so you can quickly find your way around.

4. Common Interests

At the start of term you will get to know new people and they will get to know you. It can be exciting and a bit scary meeting new people and finding out what they are interested in. A great activity to help you identify your own interest is to draw a shield on a piece of paper and add three things to the shield that you feel represent you. If you like animals, you could draw your favourite animal. If you like music you could draw some musical notes, for example. New people like to get to know what you are interested in to see if you have things in common. If you are willing to talk about your interests and show interest in what other people like doing, you will find it easier to talk to them and you will get to know them more quickly.

5. Similarities

When pupils go up to secondary school they may notice quite a lot of similarities to their old school. The building may be a similar age and the uniform may look similar. When you go and visit your new school you can look out for the similarities. See how many similarities you notice. When things look similar to what you are used to, this can feel reassuring.

6. Differences

Some pupils worry about the differences between their old school and their new school. They worry about the building being larger and unfamiliar. They worry about having to get to know different staff and new pupils.

Some pupils worry about having to go to different classrooms to be taught by lots of teachers. It is perfectly natural to feel a bit anxious about having to cope with so many different things at once.

Most schools offer the new pupils the chance to visit the school a few times before the start of the new year.

Don't feel embarrassed to ask questions, because if you find out what you need to about your new school, you are less likely to feel worried.

7. Safe Places

Some pupils worry about falling out with other pupils and feeling unsafe. It can help you feel calmer knowing that there are safe places to go if you have this problem. Have a look in your new school when you visit, to see where some safe places are that you could go to if you were feeling worried. Some schools have a quiet room and others have a member of staff you can speak to when you have a problem. You may be able to go to their office.

Every school is different, but every school has somewhere you can go if you need help. Knowing this can really help you to feel less concerned.

8. Safe People

When you arrive at your new school you will soon learn who the people are that you can go to if you have a problem. Your form tutor is usually a great person to talk to. There may be teaching assistants that help you that you feel you can trust too. All children are different. You will get to know people and will soon decide who the staff are that you feel you can trust to help you if you have a problem. Don't feel silly or embarrassed if you do need to talk to someone. The staff at the school are used to helping pupils feel happier in school. They will be pleased that you felt that you were able to ask them for help.

9. Question And Answer Postcards

If you have a lot of questions, maybe you could get some blank postcards or post-its and write a question on them. Some schools have a box where you can post your comments and questions and your tutor can answer them. Even if your school hasn't got this, you can give your postcards to your teacher and I am sure that they will be happy to answer them.

It is good to write your questions down when they pop into your head. If you don't, you may forget to ask your tutor next time you see them.

10. Visit

It is a great idea to visit your new school. Most schools offer taster days where they let you come in and look around the school, join some lessons and maybe stay for lunch. Visits give you the opportunity to get to know the staff and other children. By walking round the school, you will start to work out where everything is. You will find the toilets, the classrooms, the place you go for lunch and the assembly hall. You will be able to look outside at the playing field or playground.

Once you know more about your new school, you are likely to feel less anxious and more prepared for your first full day.

11. Research

You can go online and research your new school. They probably have a website and this is likely to tell you more about the staff and the lessons. Most school websites have photos of the buildings and they usually have a welcome message from the head teacher. You may be able to find out more about the staff and there may even be photos of some of the classrooms.

You can look up the school on Google Maps to find out exactly where the school is and how far away it is from your home.

If you look at the map on 'Street View' you may be able to see a photo of the school and the surrounding areas. This will help you to become more used to the school and what it looks like.

12. Photos

When you visit the school you may be able to take photographs of the building to help you remember what it looks like. Check with the school staff and ask their permission before getting out a camera or phone and taking a picture.

If you Google the school, you may find there are some photos of staff and buildings available online.

Some school websites have photos of the pupils and staff that you can look at too.

13. Timetables

When you go and visit your new school, you can ask them if they have a timetable so you can work out when your lessons will be and how long they will last. Sometimes, there is a copy of the school timetable on their website, so it is worth looking there to see if you can find one. It is a good idea to have a look at the timetable so you can work out how long the lessons will be and when assemblies will be held.

14. Lists

Some pupils are worried that they will forget things. If you are worried about this, you could start using a list to write down the most important things you need to remember. If you write things on a list, you can tick them off your list when a task is completed or you can cross them out. Keeping a list can stop people getting anxious about forgetting important things on their first day.

15. Diary

It can be a great idea to keep a diary. You can write down all your thoughts and feelings in a diary. If you are worried about something, you can write that in your diary too. If you have a great idea, you can put that in your diary.

The lovely thing about diaries is you can read back over them later and see how much things have changed.

If you write about what you think your first day at school will be like, you can read what you put after your first day is over and you can see if your thoughts were accurate.

16. Lunch

A lot of pupils get worried about the thought of lunchtime at secondary school. They worry that the lunch hall will be too big and too noisy. They worry that they won't have anything to do at lunchtime and they don't know if anyone will play with them.

Every school is different, but all schools make sure that there are enough staff around to support any pupils who get lost or worried at lunchtime. It will feel a bit strange going to lunch the first time, but you will soon get used to it.

You can ask about lunch times if you do attend a taster day. The staff will be happy to tell you where you will go for lunch. They will let you know about any activities or clubs that are available too.

17. Break

In primary schools they usually have a lunch break and two other breaks. In secondary school there is usually one morning break and one lunch break. This can take a bit of getting used to. Primary schools tend to have play equipment on the playground and while secondary schools tend to have less play equipment, a lot of them do have equipment such as balls and bikes which they get out sometimes.

18. Rules

Every school has its own rules. Some classes agree a set of rules to follow on their first day. The school will explain any rules that they have. They will also explain what happens if rules are broken. Don't be afraid to ask questions if you don't understand something or you would like them to let you know more.

Rules are intended to make things fair for everyone.

19. Homework

A lot of children worry that they will get a lot of homework when they start secondary school. Some primary schools give out quite a lot of homework too, but some don't expect pupils to complete much homework at all.

When you first start at secondary school they will explain how much homework you are expected to complete. They may give you a homework planner where you can write in what homework you have each day and when it needs to be handed in to your teacher.

Secondary schools know that primary pupils aren't used to having much homework so they are likely to start off gently by giving you just a little bit to complete in your first week. They will gradually increase the amount as you get used to doing it.

The key is to get work done as soon as you can after it is set. If you do this, you are less likely to get left behind. It is not a nice feeling having lots of homework that all needs to be handed in on the same day because you have been putting off completing it.

If you do a little bit of homework each school day, you won't have work to do at the weekends.

20. Vocabulary

Some pupils get confused at all the new words that they have to learn when they start secondary school. Primary pupils may have studied science but may not have been expected to know about physics, chemistry and biology, for example. History and geography may be known as humanities. Don't worry if you come across a word you don't understand. Ask another pupil or member of staff and they will be able to explain what the new words mean.

21. Subjects

When you start secondary school you may start to learn new subjects. This can be exciting but some pupils worry that it might be hard to start learning something new, right from the beginning. If you are worried about this, think back to when you started school. You had to start learning new subjects then and now you know a lot about them. The same will happen when you start secondary school. Things will seem a bit strange and different at first, but you will soon get more familiar with things.

Another thing that primary pupils find strange is having to move from class to class and get taught by a variety of teachers. In most primary schools pupils are taught most of their lessons by one teacher. Even if you are used to having one teacher most of the time, you are likely to have had different teachers if your teacher was off sick one day. Some primary schools move pupils into different groups for maths and English. If your school did that, you are used to having at least one other teacher each week.

If you look back at your time in primary school, you may have had a new teacher at the start of each year. You got used to them in the end didn't you?

It may take time to learn the new teachers' names but you will get used to them very soon.

22. Timeline

If you are starting to get worried about coping at secondary school it can be helpful to use a timeline to help you remember how many new things you have learnt in your life so far.

Born-----------1-----2------3----4-----5------6----10

The numbers are how old you were. Write under them when you began to walk, talk, feed yourself, run, started school etc.

Look back at all the things you didn't know how to do but you do now. You coped with all those new things. You were probably scared and excited about starting primary school, but you coped. Knowing this can help you to cope with feeling a bit worried about starting secondary school.

23. Aims

It can be a good idea to have an idea of what you aim to achieve at secondary school. You might want to make more friends. You might want to feel more confident about talking to school adults. You might aim to get better at handwriting. If you have a few aims that you would like to achieve this can help you to feel more willing to get involved. You have a good idea about what you want to achieve and so you can focus on this when you get there.

24. Problem Solving

You might be worrying about what to do if you have problems in your new school. A great way of solving problems is to use The Problem Solving Cycle.

First, you write down your problem.

An example of this might be:

'I don't understand fractions in maths.'

Next, you make a list of possible solutions.

In this case you could:

Ask a friend to help you by explaining what to do

Ask a parent for help

Ask the maths teacher for help

Go online and see if there is anything to help you

Once you have a list of possible solutions, look at each one carefully and see which one looks the best.

Try out your chosen solution.

In this example, the pupil decided to tell their maths teacher.

You can then decide if your solution worked.

In this example, the maths teacher was able to explain again and this time the pupil understood.

If your solution works, then you no longer have that problem. If it didn't work you can go back to your list and see if there is another solution to try. You can ask your friends if they have any more solutions you can add to your list. Keep trying the solutions until one works.

Knowing about The Problem Solving Cycle can really help you to stay calm in a crisis.

25. Goals

It can be a good idea to have one or two goals that you would like to achieve in the first week at school. Good goals could include trying to get to know more people and being brave enough to ask questions in class.

It doesn't matter what your goals are but if you have a goal you can divide it up into small manageable steps and this can really help you to achieve your goal.

With the example of getting to know more people, you could divide this goal up into chunks. You could decide that you are going to talk to one new person each day. If you managed to do that, you will have spoken to five new people in the first week.

It can be scary plucking up courage to do this at first, but if you take a deep breath, go up to a friendly looking person and ask them something about themselves, they are likely to reply and you will have taken that important first step towards achieving that goal.

26. Old Friends

When you leave primary school you sometimes find that some of your friends are going to other secondary schools so you may worry that you will lose touch with them.

This doesn't have to happen if you make the effort to stay in touch with them.

You might be able to carry on playing online games with them or if you keep their phone number you can phone them up and chat to them sometimes. You may be able to meet them in the holidays and weekends.

You could talk to your parents and ask them if you can meet up with your old friends sometimes.

27. New Friends

While it is nice to stay in touch with old friends, it is a great idea to make some new friends when you go to secondary school. It is lovely to have people you get on with and enjoy talking to at school.

When you first start at the school have a look around and see which pupils seem fun and friendly. You can make the first move by going up to them and asking them something about themselves. Maybe you could ask what school they used to go to or you could ask them about their hobbies.

It can be hard to approach new people if you are shy, but if you are friendly other people are likely to respond well to you.

28. Clubs

A lot of secondary schools run clubs that you can attend. It can be a good idea to join some clubs. They may give you something to do at lunch or they may be run after school. They will give you a chance to have fun and meet new people. You may be able to learn a new skill.

If you are told about some clubs in school and you are interested, don't let nerves put you off. Sign up, take a deep breath and go along.

If you don't enjoy the first session, try and attend another session as you may like it more the next time.

29. Tests

Some pupils worry about tests when they start at secondary school. They may have heard that there are more tests at secondary school than there were at primary school. They may be concerned that they won't cope with the pressure.

Don't worry about tests.

When a teacher teaches you a new topic, they sometimes give you a short test at the start to see what you know about it. Later on, they may test you again to see how much you have learnt. The teacher uses this information to work out what they still need to teach and which parts you have already understood.

That is why there is no need to worry about these tests. They are intended to help the teacher to make sure they are giving you the right information so that you can progress. In a way, the test is more of a test of the teacher than it is a test of you.

30. Careers

Some pupils know what they want to be when they grow up. Other pupils have not decided what they want to do when they leave school. It doesn't matter if you have made up your mind or not. When you join secondary school, you will be taught lots of different subjects and as you get older you will be given advice and support to assist you in deciding what subjects to take for GCSE's or other exams. At around Year 10, you may be able to have some work experience which may help you to start deciding what you want to do in your future career. You don't have to make your mind up for a long time though. Finding out about the world of work is an exciting and sometimes daunting experience. Try not to dwell on it for long. Keep looking out and listening for jobs that appeal to you so that when the time comes you will know what you would like to aim for.

31. Active Listening

A lot of pupils moving up to secondary school worry that nobody will listen to them. They fear that they aren't cool enough so other pupils won't like them. They worry that they don't know any good jokes and don't really know what to say to other pupils to ensure that they listen to them.

If this applies to you, I am going to let you know a great way to ensure other people want to spend time with you. Become an active listener.

What is active listening?

Active listening is where you fully listen to what the other person is saying without jumping in with comments before they have finished speaking.

When someone realises that you are genuinely interested in what they have to say and that they are listening carefully, they feel happy. If you become a really good listener, the chances are good that the other pupils will also listen to what you have to say.

You don't need to have lots of jokes ready or to have cool things to say. Most people really appreciate being listened to.

They also like it if you ask questions when they have finished speaking asking them more about what they have been talking about. By doing this you are showing that you are interested in what they have to say and people find this appealing.

Try it for yourself and see how it makes people more willing to be around you and listen to you.

32. E Safety

When people start secondary school they meet new people. Sometimes they add these new people as friends on social media. This is fine but if you decide to add new people, make sure you have good privacy settings and make sure you don't give away too many personal details about yourself online.

If someone starts being unkind to you on social media be willing to report and block them.

Pupils worry that they will be bullied online. If you are bullied online this can be a very unpleasant experience.

Some pupils make nasty comments about other pupils online and this message gets shared from person to person.

If you receive an unkind message about someone else, resist the urge to share the post or add anything unkind yourself.

If used sensibly, the internet can really be fun for pupils but you need to make sure you are safe online.

Make sure you don't start looking up things that are inappropriate for your age group. Doing this can get you into trouble.

If you accidentally open an attachment that makes you feel uncomfortable or unsafe, be honest and tell an adult that you trust straight away. They can help to make sure that you are safe and protected.

Support is available on the internet.

Childnet offer good advice on this:

https://www.childnet.com/?gclid=Cj0KCQjwtr_mBRDeARIsALfBZA7D3flWi6yiQtPlffJAR98WJp9MncRi3_IZ__sQbpXrKSRybFa_gWcaAqdsEALw_wcB

33. Transport

When pupils move up to secondary school they sometimes have to start using public transport or they have to travel further to get to school. Some pupils are happy with this but for some pupils, using public transport can be scary at first if they are not used to it.

It is a good idea to go on buses and trains with your parents or carers a few times to get used to travelling this way.

You can even travel the route that you will be taking to get to school so it doesn't seem unfamiliar on your first school day.

If you have a longer journey to get to secondary school, you can bring things to entertain you on the journey. Maybe you can listen to music on an MP3 player or you have a game you can play.

Maybe you can bring a book with you if you are able to read while travelling. Some people feel travel- sick if they travel and read but reading can really pass the time for some people.

34. Sleep

A lot of pupils don't get enough sleep. When they get home from school they feel that they have limited time to do the things they enjoy, so they tend to stay up late watching TV or playing computer games.

The trouble with this is that as pupils reach secondary school age, they need a lot of sleep to help them to grow and develop. Research has suggested that teenagers need at least 9 hours sleep per night but many teenagers don't have anything like this amount of sleep.

If you don't get enough sleep, you are likely to feel tired and grumpy a lot of the time and this can affect your learning.

Some pupils have trouble getting to sleep. Sometimes this is because they have too many drinks containing caffeine. Caffeine can really keep you awake at night. Most people realise that there is caffeine in coffee and tea, but they don't realise it is in fizzy drinks such as coca cola.

Screen time before bed can affect sleep too. It is a good idea to stop looking at computers, tablets and TVs at least 30 minutes before trying to sleep.

If you make sure you get enough sleep, you are likely to feel much happier and full of energy when you go to school.

35. Work Life Balance

You may have heard people talking of the importance of achieving a good work-life balance. This means that we all need to make sure we spend enough time working and enough time relaxing by doing the things we enjoy in order to do well and feel happy.

Some people don't get enough work done and fall behind. This causes them to feel worried and tense.

Some people overwork and don't do many things they enjoy. This isn't good for them either.

If you do enough work to do a good job and you make time to do things you love then this means that you have managed to achieve a good work-life balance.

If you find that you are not doing enough homework and you are starting to get into trouble at school because of this then the best thing to do is plan to do a little bit more homework each day. That way, you are likely to catch up slowly but surely and you will still have time to do the things you enjoy.

If you find you are overdoing work and are having no time to have fun then make sure you allow yourself a little bit of time to have fun each day and you will soon start to feel better.

36. Overwhelm

Some pupils get very stressed when they think about all the new things they will have to cope with when they start their new school. When you feel you have too many things to think about and you are feeling worried and tense about this, the chances are that you are feeling overwhelmed.

A good way to cope with this is to write a list of all the things that you are thinking about. Getting all of these thoughts on the paper can help you feel less overwhelmed.

You can look at your list and see if you can take any action to help you feel less worried.

For example, if you wrote down that you are worried that you will lose touch with your friends you can think about possible solutions to make sure that you don't lose touch. Maybe you can arrange to meet up with them in the holiday?

There are usually things you can do to reduce your worries if you tackle one problem at a time.

This can help you to feel less overwhelmed.

37. Affirmations

If you feel worried about going to your new school it can be helpful to use affirmations to help you feel calmer. An affirmation is a statement you say to yourself that can help you to feel more confident.

You can tell yourself, 'I am doing my best and my best is good enough.'

You could say, 'I am ready to start my new school!'

Affirmations can help you to feel happier about things.

38. Try New Things

One of the things pupils worry about when they leave primary school is that they are going to have to try a lot of new things. The thought of having to step out of your comfort zone can be frightening.

Think back to the times when you tried things for the first time. A few years ago, you started primary school. That was a new experience for you at the time and you coped with that.

You have learnt to do a lot of things so far I your life and you have got used to lots of new experiences.

Knowing this can help you to feel happier. It is normal to feel nervous about trying new things.

When we worry about trying something new, we are demonstrating our 'fear of the unknown.'

It is not surprising that people worry about things that they know very little about. They worry that they may come across something that has never happened to them before and they worry how they will cope.

Try and focus on one thing at a time. If you realise that you are worrying about lots of things, write them down. Look through the list of things you are worried about and see if there is any action that you can take to help you feel calmer. Tell yourself that you will try your best with each new experience and that your best is good enough.

39. Failure

A lot of people worry about failing or getting things wrong. This can put some people off trying. If you are pushing yourself to do something difficult, new and exciting, you are bound to get things wrong sometimes. If you never get things wrong, maybe you aren't challenging yourself enough.

The way we succeed is by trying something, getting it wrong and being brave enough to keep trying until we get it right.

If something is worth doing, don't give it up if you fail the first time. Try again and again and you will get there in the end.

40. Success

Some people worry that if they do too well at something, other people will feel jealous. This can put people off showing off their talents and doing well at school.

True friends will be pleased at your success. If someone tells you they don't want to be your friend because you are better than them at something, then maybe they aren't a very good friend anyway.

There is no need to feel embarrassed. Don't let other people feeling jealous hold you back. Be willing to show your talents in school and enjoy your success.

41. Bullying

One thing pupils tend to worry about is being bullied.

Some pupils had a hard time in their old school and they worry that they will be picked on in their new school. Some pupils will be going up to secondary school with other pupils who bullied them in the past.

You don't need to worry alone. If someone picks on you in your new school, make sure that you let staff, parents or carers know about it. Bullies rely on pupils being too scared to tell anyone what is happening. When you let others know what they have done, they no longer have power over you.

Childline offers lots of useful help and advice to help you take action to stop people bullying you:

https://www.childline.org.uk/

42. Communication

When you start secondary school you will be communicating with lots of different people in lots of different ways. You will be asked questions by adults and pupils. You will be given the chance to ask questions too.

Communication comes in many forms.

We communicate verbally but we also rely on non-verbal communication including body language.

We can learn a lot from other people's body language. If someone is standing with their hands on their hips and a scowl on their face we can predict that they might not be feeling very happy.

When we are able to use people's body language to help us understand how they are feeling, we can communicate with them better.

Communicating involves speaking and listening. If you are good at both, you will become a good communicator.

43. Think Ahead

It can be good to think ahead about things that will be happening in future as long as this doesn't worry or upset you. Thinking ahead too often, can make people feel anxious.

If you find that you are spending too much time thinking about the future it is a good idea to distract yourself by carrying out an activity to take your mind off things.

If you enjoy exercise then going for a run or playing some sport can really help take your mind off things. You may prefer making some art or listening to some music. These activities can really help you focus on what is happening now and you worry less about what might happen in the future.

44. Relaxation

We all have things that we find relaxing. It is important that we spend time finding fun ways to relax. What one person finds relaxing, another person may find frustrating, so it is a good idea to experiment and find what works best for you.

There is a technique called Progressive Muscle Relaxation that can help you to relax.

Sit on a chair and start by tensing and then relaxing your hands. Next tense then relax your arms and work your way around your body tensing then relaxing each muscle. This can really help you to feel relaxed. Taking a few deep breaths can also help. Make sure you breathe in for a count of three and out for a count of four to make sure you let all the breath out. When people feel tense they have a tendency of holding their breath and this can make them feel even more tense.

45. Hobbies

Instead of sitting and worrying about things, why not try out some new hobbies? Hobbies are a great way to relax and have fun. You may have some existing hobbies that you have been neglecting. In which case why not spend some time working on those hobbies?

You can look out for new hobbies to begin too.

When you start school, you may find some of your new friends have hobbies that you might like to try.

Try something new and discover how much fun it can be.

46. Road Safety

As you get older you are given more independence. When you were younger, people may have helped you cross the road and maybe now they are expecting you to develop this skill for yourself.

It is also important to be aware of traffic when playing near roads and to make sure that you don't put yourself in danger.

NI Direct offers lots of helpful road safety advice:

https://www.nidirect.gov.uk/articles/road-safety-seven-11-year-olds

As you get older you will become more independent and you need to remember to be safe near roads. Some young people forget how dangerous roads can be and they take unnecessary risks.

Be sensible and follow the Green Cross Code when crossing roads to reduce the risk of injury.

47. Exercise

Getting enough exercise is very important. It helps you to keep fit and stay healthy. This will help you to do well in school as you will feel more alert.

Some pupils love exercise but others don't.

Try experimenting with different types of exercise to see what works for you. You may enjoy running, skipping, swimming or playing a certain type of sport.

You may have friends who would be happy to exercise with you or maybe you can ask a family member to join you.

You don't need to exercise for hours. A few minutes exercise a day is better than nothing.

If you find a sport or another form of exercise you enjoy, you are more likely to keep doing it. Experiment and see what type of exercise works for you. `

48. Staff Roles

When you start your new school it can be confusing to meet all the staff and work out what their different roles are. There will be subject teachers and you are likely to have a form tutor and there will probably be teaching assistants there to help you too. You may find that there are other staff that work at the school. There could be counsellors or therapists who are there to help you if you need them. Don't be afraid to ask what someone's role is. They will be able to explain what their job is and how they can support you.

Once you have been at your new school for a little while, you will start to get more familiar with the staff that work there and what they do.

49. Feelings and Emotions

When pupils think about starting a new school they can feel a mixture of emotions. They can feel happy and excited one minute and worried the next. If this happens to you, try not to be worried about it. It is normal to have a mixture of emotions about moving from one school and starting another. Try talking to other people about how you are feeling. Your friends are probably feeling the same and adults in your life were young once and can probably remember feeling like that too.

Knowing that other people feel like they are on a rollercoaster of emotions can really help.

50. Getting Stuck

There will be times when you worry about how you will cope if you are asked to do something and you get stuck.

We all get stuck and make mistakes sometimes.

Be open about how you are feeling and people can support you through these fears. Think about the times you got stuck before and how you manged to work out what to do.

If you do get stuck at school there will be lots of people there who can help you. Don't be afraid to ask for the help you need. We all feel a bit awkward asking for help at first but there will be staff at school whose job is to help you to sort out this kind of difficulty. They will be happy to help you.

51. Helping Others

One way to feel better about yourself and your own worries is to offer to help other people. By listening to other people and offering to help, you can take your mind off your own worries. Distracting yourself from your worries in this way is a great idea as you are doing something good to help someone else at the same time as feeling better yourself.

If someone you know seems worried about something, you can ask them if there is something that they are worried about that you can help them with.

By showing that you are willing to help them, they may decide to let you know what is worrying them.

If they do tell you what is the matter, make sure you listen carefully to the problem they have. Once they have told you the problem, see if both of you can think of possible solutions to the problem. They can choose a solution to try and then see if this has resolved their problem.

If they still have the problem, you can help them look at another solution to try and see if that helps. It may be that they have a big problem that you feel they might need an adults help with. If this is the case, be honest with them and help them decide which adult would be the best person to talk to.

By listening to them and offering to help them in this way, you will have made things a lot easier for them. Well done!

52. Risk Taking

Sometimes we need to take risks to make progress. I don't mean people should put themselves in danger by doing something silly. What I mean is, in order to make progress, we need to push ourselves a bit. If we are brave enough to step out of our comfort zone and try a task we find a little difficult, we may make mistakes at first but if we keep going we are much more likely to succeed.

People can be scared to try things they find difficult as they don't want to risk looking silly if they get it wrong. If you are willing to risk trying new things and work that little bit harder at something, you are much more likely to succeed. Good luck!

53. Work Experience

When you have attended secondary school for a few years you may be encouraged to try some work experience. You may be invited to work in a shop or office for a few days, for example.

It is good to have some experience of what it is like to have a job. If you do this then you will feel more confident about applying for a job of your own when the time comes.

Secondary school aims to offer you new experiences, to help you feel more confident about growing up and getting more independent.

Growing up can be both exciting and a little frightening as you are asked to try new things. The more you try and make the most of the opportunities you are offered the more fun your school experience is likely to be.

54. Options

You may have heard that after being at secondary school for a few years you will be asked to choose options to study in Year 10 and 11. At the end of year 11 you usually sit exams before leaving Key Stage 4.

You are still asked to study what are known as core subjects such as English, maths and science but you may be asked to choose between other subjects such as art, music and drama.

You don't need to think about which options you are going to choose yet but it can be helpful to understand a bit more about what happens later in secondary school.

When the time comes, you will be give lots of help to decide which subjects and which exams are right for you.

55. Loneliness

Some pupils worry that they will feel lonely at secondary school. Maybe they had lots of friends at primary school who are going to another school next.

It is only natural to be a little concerned about this, but don't get too worried.

There will be staff to support you at school. You can talk to them.

There will probably be clubs and activities that you can participate in and if you try your best to listen to other pupils and be friendly, they are likely to respond well to you and you should soon make new friends.

Childline can help if loneliness does turn out to be a problem for you:

https://www.childline.org.uk/info-advice/your-feelings/feelings-emotions/loneliness-isolation/

56. Long Days

Some pupils worry that the school day is longer in secondary school. Some lessons can go on for longer too.

When you start secondary school you are taking in so much new information that you can feel tired at the end of the day. Don't worry about this. You will soon adjust to your new timetable. Most schools try not to give out too much homework in the first week to help you to adjust. Try and make sure you get enough sleep. That will help you to stay alert during your first week.

You are getting older and so your stamina is building up. You will soon get used to the longer lessons and will benefit from being able to spend time studying interesting topics in your new school.

57. Possessions

When you go to secondary school listen to any advice the staff give you about what you can bring into school. There is no point in bringing in things they have told you not to bring in. It is also important to make sure that your possessions are clearly labelled so that they can be returned to you if they get lost. Don't bring in precious toys that could get lost or broken.

58. Asking For Help In Class

When you start at the new school, don't be afraid to ask for help if you need it in class. Some pupils have an Education, Health and Care Plan. (EHC Plan) This plan lists extra support and help they may be entitled to.

If you have an EHC plan you may be entitled to extra staff support, for example.

Even if you don't have an EHC plan there are likely to be some school staff available to help you if you get stuck. They can't help if they don't know that you are having trouble. Be honest and let them know you don't understand the work and you need some extra help.

If you are finding it hard to ask for the help you need, let your parents or carers know so they can talk to the school on your behalf.

Once the staff know that you need more help, they should find ways of making sure that you receive the help that you need.

59. Special Needs and Difficulties

Lots of pupils have Special Needs and they can do very well if they receive the help and support that they need. Some pupils have physical needs and difficulties and some pupils have hidden difficulties. If someone has ADHD or Attention Deficit Hyperactivity Disorder, for example. They may find it hard to concentrate in class. You can't look at someone and see they have ADHD which is why it can be described as a hidden difficulty.

If you have Special Needs, it is important that the school know this so that they are able to support you properly. You may be given an Education, Health and Care Plan or EHC plan. This is put in place to make sure staff know how you learn best, to make sure that you get the right help and support to progress.

Don't feel embarrassed or worried about any Special Needs you may have. A lot of pupils will have Special Needs and it is the school's responsibility to ensure that you receive the help you need.

60. Strengths

We all have strengths and we can use them to help us progress. Some people are very creative, other people are very patient, while other people are very dedicated. We can use our strengths to help us and we can benefit from the strengths of our friends too.

It is very helpful if you have an idea of what your strengths and talents are and it is lovely if you are able to share them with others.

61. Timeline

If you get overwhelmed by all the things you need to do before starting the new school, it can be very helpful to use a timeline to help you to make plans.

Start by drawing a line horizontally across the page and you can put a mark at the start of the line. This represents now. At the end of the line you can add another mark. This represents starting the school on the first day.

Now I.........................I........................I........................I Start

In this example, the pupil planned to meet up with friends. They knew they were going on holiday and they decided to get a diary to write down their worries, thoughts and feelings in. They can plot these actions on the timeline.

Timelines can really help you to plan out the things you need to do and once an event has taken place you can tick it off.

Try it for yourself and see if it helps you.

62. Be Present

When we get worried about things that have gone wrong in the past or we are anxious about things that might happen in the future, it is a good idea to focus on the present.

Look around you, what can you see right now?

Stay silent for 5 minutes and notice what you can hear. If you have something to eat or drink, focus fully on eating or drinking. What does the food or drink taste and smell like?

What do the clothes you are wearing feel like?

Using your senses to focus on the world as it is happening now can really help you to stop getting caught up with worrying about things too much.

63. What If?

You often hear people saying, 'What if I get lost?' 'What if nobody likes me in my new school?' 'What if I get stuck at maths?'

When people say 'What if?' they are usually worried about something going wrong in the future.

It can be reassuring to turn this around and say, 'What if I easily find my way around school?' 'What if everyone likes me in my new school?' 'What if I cope easily in maths?'

This can help our thoughts to be more balanced. We can't say for certain how things will work out but we can remind ourselves that if things do go wrong there are lots of things we can do to improve the situation. We can ask for help and we can use The Problem Solving Cycle to act on problems that have solutions. We can learn to distract ourselves when we realise we are having worries about things that can't be changed. We can distract ourselves with things we enjoy doing until our worried thoughts pass.

64. Uniform

A lot of pupils worry about wearing the new school uniform. Some pupils find certain clothes uncomfortable. Some pupils have sensory issues where a certain material feels very uncomfortable for them. If you have sensory difficulties like this, it is a good idea for your parents or carers to let your new school know. It may be that they can be flexible and offer you a suitable alternative to wear.

Some pupils just hate wearing uniform but if they wear it on the first day, they will soon get used to wearing it. In many jobs, people are expected to wear a uniform. Nurses and soldiers have a uniform that they are expected to wear, for example.

65. Socialising

Some pupils love socialising and other pupils are shy, so they find socialising hard.

If you are sociable, you are probably looking forward to meeting new people and if you are shy, you may be more nervous about the thought of getting to know new people. We are all different.

When you start school, there will be pupils who are more confident then you and pupils who are less confident than you.

If you are shy, try and be as friendly as possible but don't worry if you are too shy to talk to lots of new people. Take your time, and you will gradually get to know the other pupils in your year group.

66. Taster Days

Most schools offer new pupils the chance to visit on taster days. Pupils are given the chance to look around the school, meet the staff and other pupils and you may get the chance to attend some lessons.

These taster days often take place in the summer term before the summer holiday.

If you do get invited to attend taster days, try and go along. You will learn a lot about your new school and what to expect. This should help you feel more confident.

If you are unable to attend the taster days, maybe your parent or carer can contact the school and see if you can come and visit at another time. It is a great idea to look around your new school if you can.

67. Joining In

Some pupils love joining in with group activities while others don't. Some people are very confident working in teams while others prefer working on their own.

If you don't really enjoy joining in activities, try to have an open mind and give them a try. You may find that if you give an activity a try you may enjoy it more than you think.

If you pluck up courage to try an activity for 5 minutes, you can always stop if you really need to. Having the confidence to give new things a try is a very good thing. By being brave enough to join in you will develop new skills and you may find that you have fun!

68. Bigger School

Your new school may be bigger than you are used to. Bigger can be better. There will be more pupils to choose from so there is a good chance that someone in your year could have a lot in common with you and you could become really good friends.

Bigger schools may offer more activities and clubs for you to join in.

Getting used to a bigger school will help to prepare you for the next step when you eventually leave school and go to college or get a job.

When you were little, a smaller school may have suited you better but you are older now and there is a good chance that you are ready for something a bit bigger.

69. Remembering Names

When you go to your new school you may worry that you will have a lot of names to remember. You will be introduced to a lot of staff and new pupils and it may be difficult to remember all the names at once.

Don't worry if you do forget someone's name. Be honest and ask them to give you their name again. You can write the important names down to help you remember.

In a little while, you will look back and realise that you have learnt everyone's name and it will be hard to imagine not knowing them.

70. Losing Your Things

There is a lot you can do to reduce the risk of losing your things at school. Start off by only bringing things in that you really need. Avoid bringing in expensive toys that could get broken, lost or stolen at school. Ensure that everything is labelled so if you do lose your things there is a better chance of having them returned to you.

Most schools have a 'Lost Property' area. If you realise that something is missing, go to the Lost Property to see if it has been handed in.

When you go out on a sunny day, it can be tempting to take your jumper off and put it on the ground. If lots of pupils do this, it is easy to get clothing muddled up and lost. Instead, why not put your jumper in your locker before you go out?

It can be a good idea to make a list of the things you need to take home at the end of the day so you can tick the items off as you collect them. That way you are less likely to leave things at school and risk them getting lost.

71. Learning Support

Many schools have lots of ways to support you when you learn. Some pupils find that the classroom can get too noisy and they need somewhere quiet to go to work for a while. Some schools have nurture rooms or learning support units and you will find out about them when you visit the school.

Some schools have quiet rooms where you can go if you need to calm down.

Don't be afraid to ask staff where you can go if you need a quiet place to be. They will be very happy to help you and to let you know what facilities there are in your new school.

Most schools have some teaching assistants who can work alongside pupils in class if they need extra help. You will be told about this when you visit.

Staff are there to help you when you need them, so don't be afraid to ask for help.

72. Arguments

Some pupils worry that they will get into arguments with other pupils and this will make school difficult for them.

We all have arguments and disagreements sometimes. Try and stay as calm as possible if someone seems argumentative. Try and listen to what they say and attempt to see things from their point of view.

If you have made a mistake, be willing to apologise and if someone apologises to you, be willing to accept their apology.

Sometimes pupils worry they will get into an argument with a member of their family at home and this may affect things at school.

If this happens, let a school adult know so they are able to give you the opportunity to calm down before you go into lessons.

Remember, we all argue and sometimes we need time to calm down. If you let others know you are feeling upset, they will be able to help you feel better.

73. Fitting In

Lots of pupils worry that they won't fit in. They hate standing out and wish they could be like everybody else.

Try and see things in a different way. We are all unique with our own talents and interests. The world would be boring if we were all the same. Be proud of who you are and don't be afraid to be yourself. Most people admire those who dare to be different.

It is good to show interest in other people and enjoy doing things in groups with them, but it is wonderful if you are able to say what you think and be yourself at school. Most pupils secretly wish that they had the confidence to be themselves. It is great to feel accepted for being who you are instead of pretending to be like everybody else.

If you are brave enough to be yourself, you may help other pupils to be themselves too!

74. Resilience

When things go wrong it is very important that we develop the skills that help us to pick ourselves up and carry on. If we can learn from our mistakes and keep going we are resilient.

At secondary school you will really benefit from becoming resilient. If you are willing to try new things, get things wrong and try hard until you get things right, you will do very well.

75. Peer Pressure

Pupils sometimes worry about peer pressure.

Peer pressure is when the other pupils put pressure on you to do something that they want you to do but you don't. Peer pressure can be good if friends are encouraging you to try new things and they want you to do well, but peer pressure is not a good thing if people are putting pressure on you to do things you don't want to do.

If friends are trying to get you to do something that you know is unkind, unfair, dangerous or illegal, have the confidence to say No!

If you need to, let an adult know so they can help you to stay out of trouble.

Be willing to think for yourself and don't be pushed into doing things that you know are wrong.

76. Getting Lost

Pupils worry about getting lost in school and they also worry about getting lost on the way to school.

Once you have been to school a few times, you will be more familiar with the route. Even large schools become more familiar to you once you have been in them for a while.

It is a good idea to travel to school with someone you know at first, until you feel more confident.

Maybe you can meet a friend and walk round the school together at first.

If you get lost while out of school, ask a police officer or shop staff for support. They are trained to know how to help you if you are in trouble.

If you get lost in school, any school adult should be able to help you find your way around.

You will soon get used to your new surroundings.

77. Rewards And Sanctions

Each school has their own systems of rewards and sanctions. You will be told about them when you start your new school. Some schools have a traffic light system where pupils are green when they are behaving well, amber when they need to think about their behaviour or red when they have broken a rule.

Some schools reward pupils for good work and positive behaviour by awarding them certificates or points.

Some schools provide a room for detention or reflection. Pupils are sent to this room to think about their behaviour sometimes.

Some pupils respond well to the rewards and sanctions that are used in their school while other pupils find it hard to understand them.

If you are unclear about the system in your school, don't be afraid to ask. Staff should be able to explain the system to you.

78. Absence

It is important that you try to come into school every day unless you are ill. Research has shown that pupils who miss two weeks of education in a year are at risk of falling behind. Sometimes you can't some to school due to family difficulties or illness. When you get back you may find it hard to catch up on the work you missed. If you do find this happens to you, let someone know that you are struggling so they can help you to catch up with the work you have missed.

Some schools reward pupils for good attendance. You may receive a prize or certificate for example.

79. Trips

Pupils are often offered the opportunity to go on school trips. These trips can be educational and fun. You might feel nervous at the thought of going on a trip but don't worry. The staff are experienced at going on trips and will make sure things run smoothly.

You will be told what you need to bring on the day and you may be able to go online to research the place you are visiting. If you find out as much as you can about where you are going, you are less likely to feel nervous.

Think back to trips you have been on before, and this can help you realise that you can feel nervous and go anyway.

Talk to staff if you feel nervous, and they should be able to reassure you.

Good luck!

80. Concentration

Lots of pupils find it difficult to concentrate sometimes. Make sure you sit away from people who hjn90pare likely to distract you. If your teacher sits you next to someone you find distracting, maybe you can let them know so they can consider letting you sit somewhere else.

Try and focus on what you are being asked to do but be willing to ask if you get stuck or lose focus.

If you get distracted, don't be cross with yourself. Let staff know you have become distracted and they can explain what you need to do next.

81. Remembering Instructions

Some pupils struggle to remember instructions. If you find this difficult, it can be a good idea to use a list to write down what you need to do. If you do this, you can cross off each activity as you complete it. If you do realise you have forgotten what you need to do, don't be afraid to let staff know so they can help you to get back on track.

82. Forgetting Things

If you get to school and realise that you have forgotten something, don't worry. Let staff know and if you urgently need something they can phone home and make arrangements for it to be sent in. Most things are less important and you will be able to get by without needing to go home or have things brought in.

A good way to help you remember things is to keep a diary. You can write down the things you need to bring in on the right day and if you get into the habit of checking your diary regularly it can remind you of the things you need to do.

It takes time to introduce a new system. It is worth sticking with this approach to see if it can help you to be better prepared for school. Good luck!

83. Stages of Development

We all develop at different rates. Some pupils enter secondary school very maturely but others will become more mature in time.

Puberty takes place usually between the ages of 12 and 16 so your body will change shape at a different rate to some of your friends.

People learn at different rates too. You may find some subjects more difficult than others. Your friends may find other subjects difficult.

You will find that you learn at different rates yourself. You may be learning rapidly for a few weeks and then you feel that your rate of learning has slowed down for a while. Don't worry about this.

If you get stuck in your learning, ask your teacher for help and they can suggest strategies to help you learn.

84. Fairness

Some pupils get very upset if they think things are unfair. They may see one of their friends being treated differently from them, for example.

Everyone is equal, but sometimes people do need to be treated differently to help them learn and progress. Some pupils need more adult help than others. This may appear unfair but staff aim to promote independence as much as possible so if they think you can complete a task alone, they will encourage you to do so. If your friend needs extra help, they may receive it.

If you see some pupils being treated differently, try and understand that they may have learning needs that you don't know about. They may need extra help. This does not mean that the teacher likes them more than you. It is down to offering individual pupils the right amount of help.

85. Uniqueness

Remember you are unique. There is only one YOU. Be proud of your gifts and talents. Try not to compete with other people. They have their skills and you have yours. If you can learn to accept yourself as you are, you will be much happier.

The world would be a very boring place if we were all the same.

86. Self Confidence

You can achieve so much more if you have confidence in yourself. Try treating yourself as well as you treat good friends. Be kind to yourself and look after yourself well. When you accept yourself as you are you will feel more confident in your abilities and talents. This will help you feel more willing to join in with things and show other people what you can do.

87. Reports

Some pupils worry about school reports that get sent out to their parents and carers. The reports are nothing to worry about. They let your parents and carers know how you are doing in each subject and they suggest targets for you to work on. If you don't understand anything in the report, talk to your teacher so that they can explain what they mean. If you attempt to work on the targets you are set, this should help you to make even more progress.

88. Parents Evening

Parents and carers are invited into school to meet your teachers and find out how you are doing in the lessons. They will make suggestions on what you can do to improve and your parents and carers will be given the chance to ask questions and let school staff know of any worries or concerns they have. If you have something that you want them to talk about, let them know what you are worried about so that they can ask staff at school to help you.

89. Public Speaking/ Performances

Some pupils love taking part in shows and performances. They like speaking in public.

Other pupils get worried at the thought of taking part in plays and productions.

If you pluck up the courage to try it, you may find you enjoy it.

If you have a speech you have been asked to make to your class as part of your English work, try not to worry about it. You will be given lots of support. Don't worry about the other pupils possibly judging you, they will be too nervous about their own speeches to notice if you make mistakes. Take a deep breath and try your best. Your best is always good enough! If you feel nervous at the thought of taking part in a show but you like the idea, why not talk to your drama teacher and explain how you feel. They will be able to encourage you and help you feel calmer.

90. Wrong Choices

Sometimes we make mistakes.

You will make a wrong choice and things will go wrong. If this happens, the best thing that you can do is to admit it and ask for help.

It is always best to be honest when you have done something wrong. The sooner you admit it, the sooner you will be able to put things right.

There is no point in spending too long regretting things that have happened in the past.

The best thing to do is when you do something wrong, work out what you could have done differently and you will make a wiser decision next time.

91. Comparisons

There is little point in comparing yourself to other people. If we have friends who are very good at something and we aren't, it can be hard. Being jealous of other people doesn't really help you.

As long as you try your best, remember your best is good enough.

You can practice things and you can get better. It is good to improve on your own personal best but try not to spend too long feeling bad because someone you know is better than you at something. You have talents too. Work on them and be glad for your friend that they also have a talent to share with the world.

92. Priorities

If you have a lot to do, it can be a good idea to prioritise the things you have to do. Make a list of all the things you need to do and then decide which things are the most important. Make sure you have time to complete the most important things. If you have time left over, you can choose to tackle the less important things.

We all need to make sure we have enough time to eat, sleep and exercise. We all have things we need to complete, but there are only 24 hours in a day. Taking time to prioritise is time well spent as you decide what you need to achieve and learn not to worry too much about the other tasks.

93. Perspectives

We all see the world from our own point of view. If two friends get into an argument it is often because they see things differently. If we see things differently from another person we say that we are seeing things from a different perspective.

If a child wants to stay up late and their Mum wants them to go to bed, they are seeing the situation from a different perspective. Mum wants her son to get enough sleep but he want to stay up and watch TV.

If you are able to try and see things from the other person's perspective, it can help you to be kinder and more understanding towards them and they are more likely to try and understand your point of view.

Remember this next time you argue with someone. Try and see things from their point of view and you will find that you communicate better with them.

94. Body Language

If you can learn to read other people's body language, you will communicate better with them.

Imagine you want to go out with your friends at the weekend and when you get home you decide to ask your parents if you can go. You get home and both parents are sitting down looking cross. They may be frowning, for example.

If you can pick up on their body language that tells you that they are not in a good mood, you may decide to wait until they seem happier before asking if you can go out.

If you can read body language, you can choose the right moment to ask people for things. This will improve your chances of getting what you wish for.

95. Making The First Move

A lot of pupils find it hard to be the one to make the first move. They may want to join in a game but feel embarrassed to ask if they can join in. If you can be brave enough to ask people to join you in a game, you may find they are only too happy to join you. If you don't ask, you will never know.

If you have fallen out with someone, it can be tempting to leave them to approach you to apologise. Why not take a deep breath and be the one to sort things out?

If you wish someone would contact you and ask to meet up, why not be the one to approach them?

When you are brave enough to make the first move, there is a risk that the other person may say 'No' to your request. If they do, that's Ok, you haven't really lost anything and if you do ask them they may say 'Yes.'

You haven't got anything to lose!

96. Supporting Others

A great way to feel better about being at school is to try and be helpful to others. Knowing you aren't the only one to have worries about school can really help you take your mind off your own concerns. If you are at school and someone looks lost or upset, ask if there is anything you can do to help.

If you think someone is in trouble, be prepared to let staff know so that they can give them the help that they need.

97. Thoughts Pass

It can be very helpful to remember that no matter how horrible our thoughts can be sometimes, they will eventually pass. If you realise you are thinking worrying thoughts about school you can gently remind yourself that while you may be having some upsetting thoughts now, they will soon pass. Knowing this can help you to feel better.

Sometimes you realise that you are worried about something that you can do something about. If that is the case, use The Problem Solving Cycle to help you to decide on possible solutions to your difficulties.

If you realise that your worries are about things you can't change, it can be good to distract yourself by doing something you enjoy to take your mind off things. Try this for yourself and see how helpful it can be.

98. School Support

If you do have difficulties at school, don't be afraid to ask for help. The staff there should be able to help you or they will find the right person to help you.

Some pupils benefit from having someone to talk to regularly. There may be a school counsellor who you can talk to. Their job is to listen to you and help you to overcome your anxieties, one step at a time.

Don't feel embarrassed to ask for the help you need.

99. Online Support

There are a lot of good websites available to help you with your difficulties. Make sure that the sites you visit really are helpful and are giving you good advice. If you are not sure about a site, ask a parent, carer or school staff member for their opinion as some sites are better than others.

I have mentioned Childline in this book. Childline is a great place to start. They offer lots of support and advice on a wide variety of issues. Never feel that you are alone. There is always someone willing to listen to you and help you.

100. Support Services

Sometimes families need help from support services such as Social Services. If your family needs help, this is nothing to feel ashamed about. Help is there to support the people who need it.

Health professionals such as doctors and nurses may also be needed to help you or a member of your family.

We are all entitled to receive the help we need to stay safe, be healthy and learn.

I hope this book has helped you to feel happier about starting secondary school.

Good luck!

Glossary:

Accurate - correct

Achieve- be successful

Aims - goal

Alternative – another possibility

Appealing - desirable

Argumentative – falling out with

Caffeine – stimulant in drinks

Careers - jobs

Challenging - testing

Comfort Zone – where you feel safe

Concerned - worried

Confident – feeling able

Confusing - unclear

Counsellor – someone who helps people with their problems

Courage - bravery

Crisis – emergency situation

Daunting - worrying

Dwell – keep thinking about

Dedicated – devoted to

Detention – staying in at break

Ensure – make sure

Entitled - allowed

Facilities - equipment

Familiar – used to

Focus – a point to concentrate on

Frustrating - annoying

GCSE – a type of exam

Genuinely - truthfully

Gradually - slowly

Humanities – History and Geography

Inappropriate – not suitable

Independence – doing it on your own

Manageable - achievable

Neglecting – leaving out

Peer – someone your age

Permission - allowed

Predict – what you think might happen

Present - Now

Pressure – being persuaded to

Privacy Settings – users control who can see it

Progressive – happening in stages

Promote - support

Puberty – when teens bodies mature

Reassure – help someone feel better

Represent – appears like

Research - investigate

Resist – try not to

Responsibility – your duty

Sanctions - punishments

Sensory – affecting your senses

Similar – almost the same as

Socialising – mixing with others

Solutions - answers

Stamina – building yourself up

Strategies - techniques

Timeline – a way of measuring time

Technique - method

Therapist – like a counsellor

Tutor – like a teacher

Unique – only one of its kind

29065865R00028

Printed in Great Britain
by Amazon